sew your own Bean Bag Friends

EVERYTHING YOU NEED BUT THE BEANS!

Written by Jill Bryant
Illustrated by chum mcleod

Somerville House, U.S.A.
New York

Copyright © 1998 Somerville House Books Limited

All rights reserved. This publication may not be reproduced or transmitted in whole or in part in any form or by any means — electronic or mechanical, including photocopy, recording or any information storage and retrieval system — without written permission from the Publisher, except by a reviewer who wishes to quote brief passages for inclusion in a review or by an individual user who wishes to replicate the patterns and/or birth certificates solely for his or her own personal use in fabricating the projects intended by this publication.

ISBN 1-58184-000-4   B C D E F G H I J

Printed in the U.S.A.

Pattern Creators: Catherine Heard and
                  Bonnie McTaggart
Designer: Michael Gray, Fiwired.com
Photographer: Tracy Clare Photography

Note:
There is enough material for three **Friends**, but (yeah!) there are four patterns.

Somerville House, USA is distributed by
The Putnam & Grosset Group, N.Y., N.Y.

Published in Canada by Somerville House Publishing,
a division of Somerville House Books Limited
3080 Yonge Street, Suite 5000
Toronto, ON
M4N 3N1

Refill Packs

You can make more **Friends** by ordering a refill pack, featuring a Dalmatian print, orange, and royal blue fabric, from Somerville House Books Limited, 3080 Yonge Street, Suite 5000, Toronto, ON, M4N 3N1, Fax (416) 488-5506, e-mail: SOMBOOKS@GOODMEDIA.COM
Eyes and noses are available at craft stores, fabric stores, and dressmaker supply stores.

Learn to Sew

Bean Bag **Friends** make great toys and gifts! The kit has enough fabric to make three furry Bean Bag **Friends**. There are four patterns to choose from: a fish, a frog, a dog, and a bear. Each one takes from two to five hours to complete. And once you make the patterns in this book, you will be ready to decorate your **Friends** and try some other sewing projects. You can buy more fabric to make more **Friends**.

You can choose which color you want to use for each Bean Bag **Friend**. We have included sample pattern layouts on page 13. Using these layouts will help you make the best use of the fabric pieces.

NOTE: Be sure to ask an adult before using needles and pins.

Find in Your Kit:
- 1 large piece of fabric
- 2 small pieces of fabric
- 2 noses with back fasteners
- 3 pairs of eyes with back fasteners

Find at Home:
- scissors
- needle
- thread to match fabric
- pins, with colored heads
- pen or chalk
- pincushion
- dried uncooked beans (approximately one cup per **Friend**.)
- fiberfill

Starting Off

Needles

Use a medium-weight, or number 8, needle to sew the velour fabric. A needle with an eye that is just large enough to pull the thread through is best. Be careful not to touch the sharp, pointed end of the needle—it hurts!

Thread

Choose thread that matches the fabric you are using. A polyester or synthetic thread works well with velour. To measure a length of thread for hand sewing, put the end of the thread in one hand and extend the spool of thread from your nose to your arm's length.

Pins

Pins with colored heads are the easiest to use. The colors make them easy to see. Pins are used to hold the pieces of fabric before you sew them together. Always keep your pins in a pincushion when you aren't using them.

Hint: Insert pins into the wrong side of the fabric to avoid pricking your finger. If you put them on the velour side, you might lose them in the soft, furry fabric.

Stitches

For all of the patterns in this book, a basic running stitch is the best one to use. Start your running stitch as below:

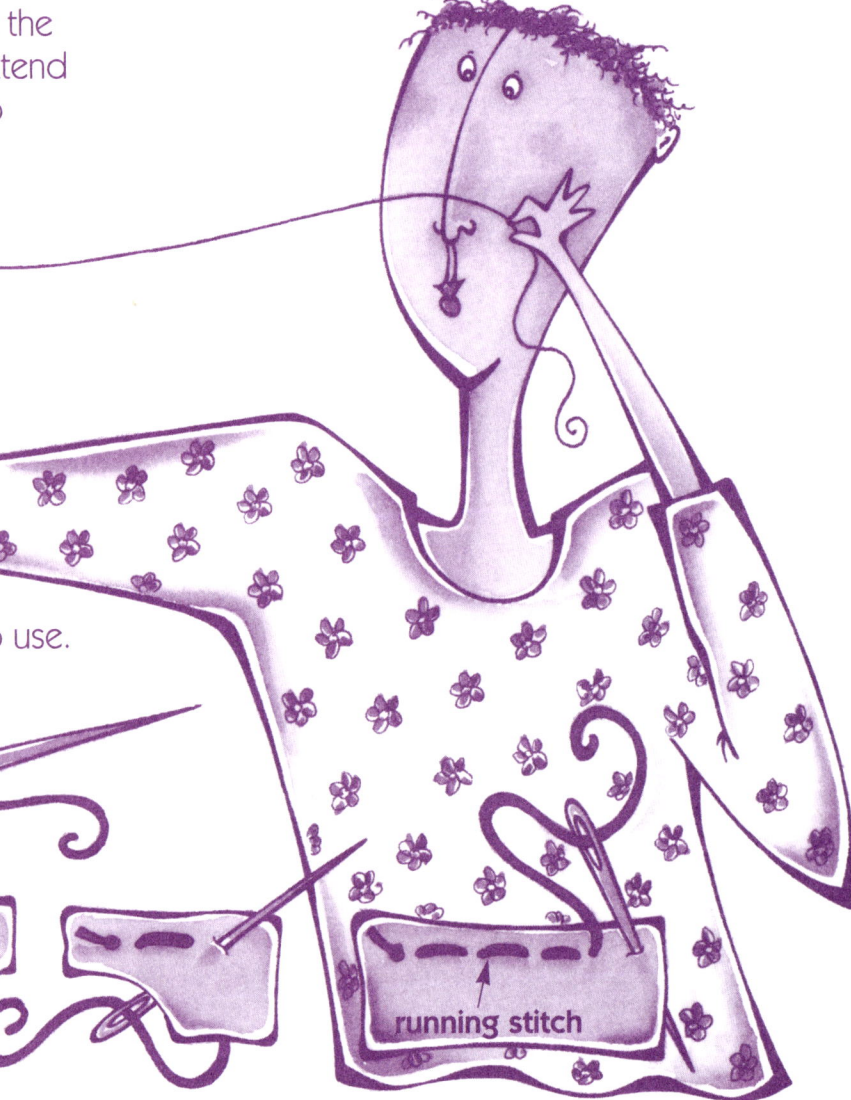

knot

running stitch

So Collectible!

Bean Bag **Friends** are great to collect.
You might want to display them in a special way. Here are some ideas:

Climber Friends

- Tie a rope to your door knob. Fasten your **Friends** to the rope with yarn or ribbon to make a **Friend** rope! Have fun finding new places to hang your growing rope.

House of Friends

- Fill a box with **Friends** and decorate the box to look like a house.

Gardening Friends

- Fill a clay flowerpot with **Friends**. Paint flowers, fruits, and vegetables on the flowerpot. Decorate the **Friends** with gardening hats that you make from felt.

Camping Friends

- Make a tent for your **Friends**. Set up the tent and go stargazing. Don't forget a flashlight!

NOTE:
There is enough material to make three **Friends**, but there are four patterns. You can make the fourth **Friend** by buying more fabric or ordering a refill pack from Somerville House (see page 2).

Get Ready... Get Set... Cut!

Right and Wrong

The "right side" of the fabric is the side that you will see on the finished Bean Bag **Friend**. It is the furry side. The "wrong side" of the fabric is the side that doesn't show on the finished **Friend**. When cutting and sewing seams, work on the wrong side of the fabric. After sewing, turn the fabric right side out. The seams are hidden!

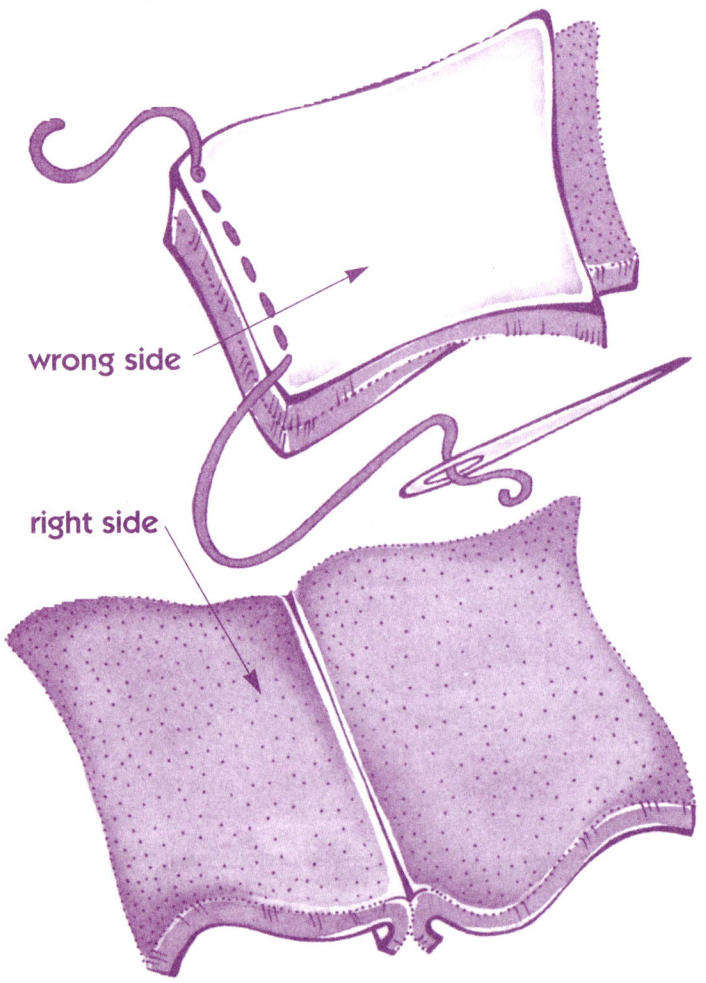

wrong side

right side

Making Pattern Pieces

- Carefully remove the pattern pages that have patterns printed on them.
- Photocopy the patterns or place tracing paper over the pages and trace the patterns with a pencil. Remember to copy more than one piece if the pattern says, "Cut 2 pieces" or "Cut 4 pieces."
- Cut out the pattern pieces.
- Pin the pattern on the "right side" of the fabric. Turn the pattern over to make a copy for the pieces that require 2 copies. This will give you a front and a back for the Fish Top Fin, for instance.
- Now you're ready to cut!
- When you finish, find an envelope to store the pattern pieces in so you don't lose them. You can use the cut-out pattern pieces again.

Scissors

Sewing scissors are very sharp! They have to be sharp to cut through heavy fabric. Ask an adult for help if you aren't used to cutting with sewing scissors. Paper scissors will not cut fabric.

Cutting

- Make sure the pattern is pinned securely to the right side of the fabric before you start cutting.
- Always cut out all the pattern pieces before you begin to sew.
- Cut slowly and carefully for the best results!

Attaching the Eyes

- Make a dot where the eye should be placed on the fabric with a pen or a piece of chalk.
- Make a little hole with a large, blunt needle through the center of the mark.
- Poke the pointed end of the eye through the fabric from the right side.
- Attach the eye's backing on the wrong side of the fabric by pressing and turning the backing around clockwise to tighten. Do this slowly and carefully. The backing is small and easy to drop.
- Repeat for the other eye.
- The noses are attached in the same way.

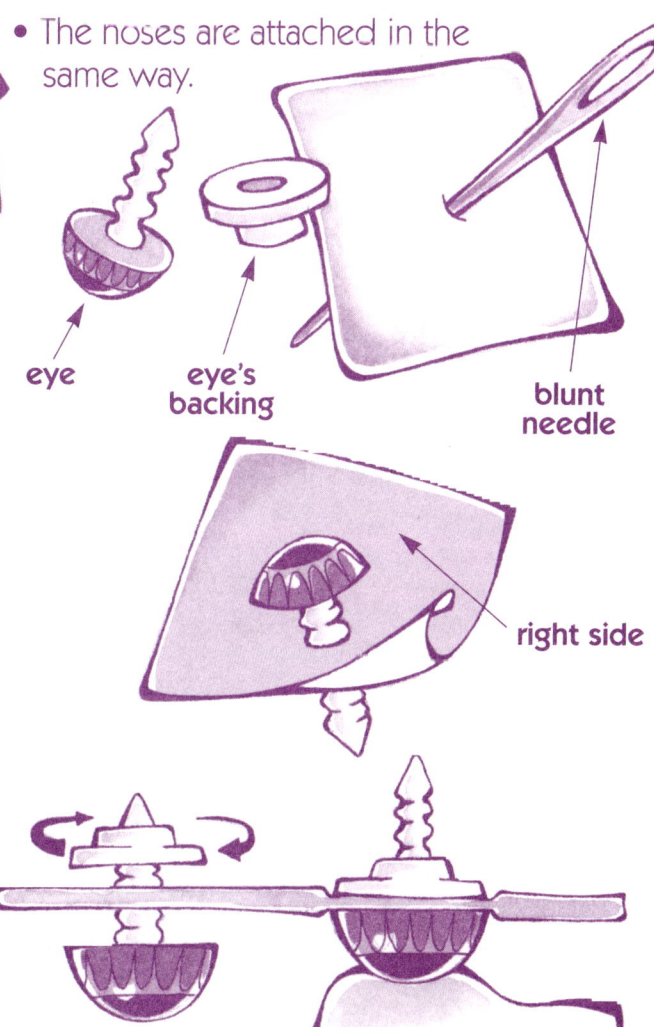

eye   eye's backing   blunt needle

right side

Cuddly Comfort

Bean Bag **Friends** make wonderful gifts. The next time you attend a birthday party, celebrate a special occasion, or visit someone in the hospital, take along a **Friend**! Decorate your finished **Friend** with things your pal especially likes. Add a hat, jewelry, or little eyeglasses.

Sew What!?

X Marks the Spot

Xs, **O**s and ✱s on the patterns show you how to place the pieces of fabric in the right position. For example, for the Swishy Fish pattern, the Fish Bottom Fin pattern piece has two **X**s on it that match up with the two **X**s on the Fish's Body pattern piece. The ✱s on the Fish's Top Fin match up with the ✱s on the Fish's Body. This prevents you from sewing the Top Fin to the bottom of the fish and the Bottom Fin to the top!

Chalk It Up!

Use a piece of chalk or a pen to copy the special marks on the patterns to the cut-out fabric pieces. Copy the **X**s, **O**s and ✱s onto the wrong side of the fabric to guide you as you sew. (You always sew on the wrong side.)

Allow Me!

A seam allowance is the distance between the edge of the fabric and the line you sew along. Seam allowances are included in all the patterns, so cut the fabric to match the pattern pieces exactly. The fabric is a little bit stretchy so pull the seams if necessary to make the pieces fit together. Remember to put the two right sides touching each other and sew on the wrong sides. When sewing the two pieces together, pin as often as needed to hold the edges securely.

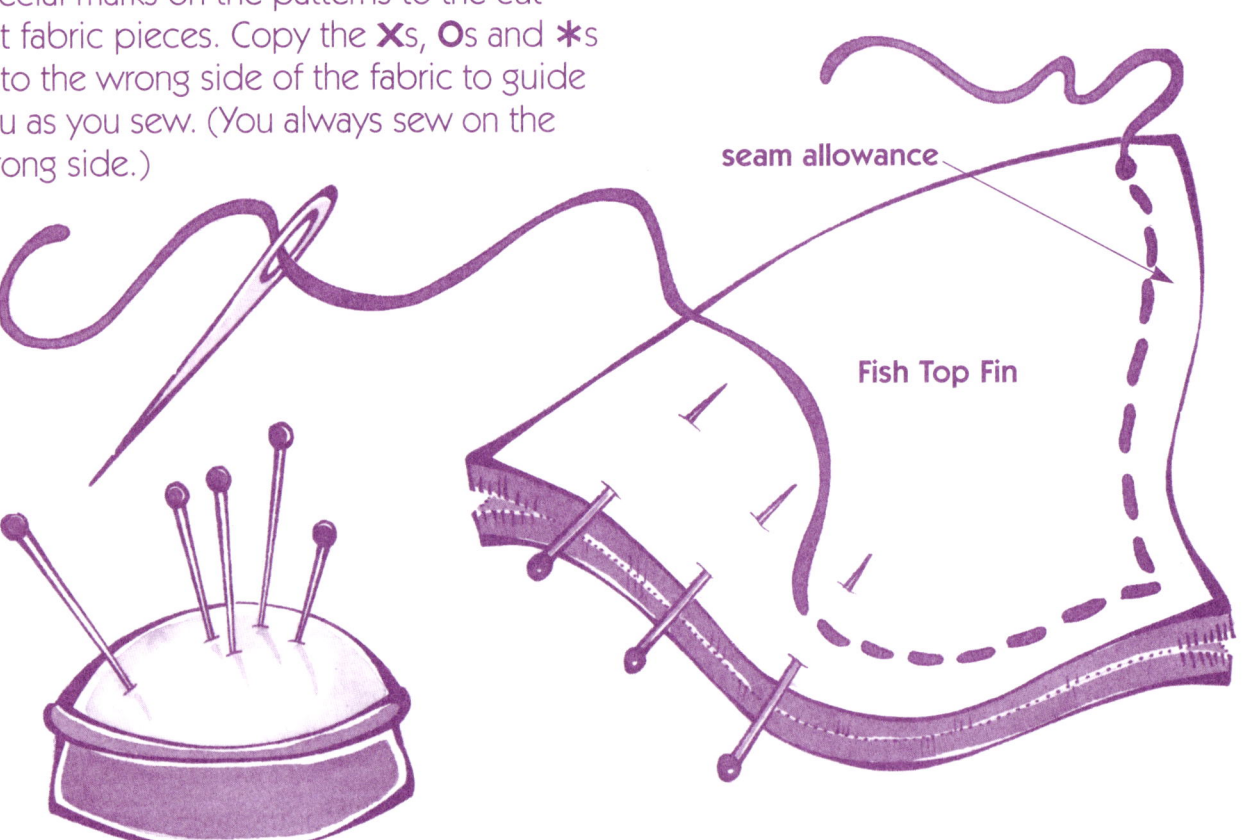

Leave a Gap!

When you sew around the body of a Bean Bag **Friend**, you have to remember to leave a little gap about 2" (5 cm) wide between where you start and stop sewing. If you have trouble remembering this, you might want to draw a line with a piece of chalk reminding you to stop sewing. Another way to remember is to place a bead-headed pin across the line of stitching so that you can't continue sewing without removing the pin.

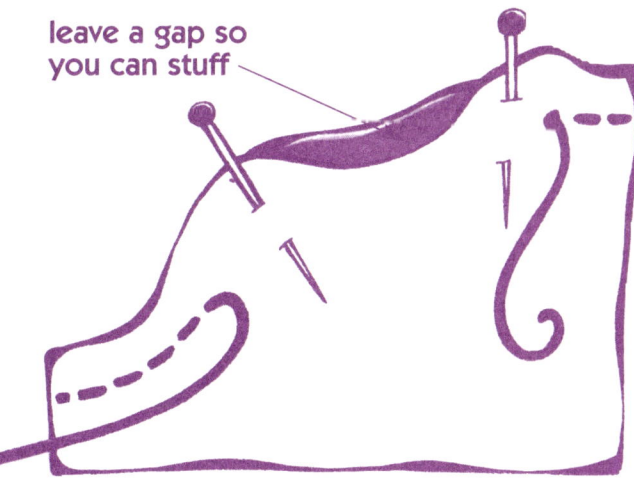

leave a gap so you can stuff

The little gap allows you to push the right side of the furry velour fabric through the gap until you have turned your Bean Bag **Friend** right side out. You might have to use a blunt pencil to turn some of the smaller areas inside out. Push the pencil firmly and gently so you don't break your stitching. Now the furry side should be on the outside and the stitches you sewed are hidden on the inside of the Bean Bag **Friend**.

Take a Break

Feeling tired? Sewing uses lots of brain power. If you're tired or frustrated, it's time to take a break. Do something active to give your brain a rest. Start sewing when you feel relaxed.

Stuff It!

Stuffing

Leave a little hole so that you can stuff your Bean Bag **Friend** with beans (dry not cooked). **Friends** look best when they are slightly floppy. Overstuffed **Friends** will weigh you down when you carry them in your backpack. Keep the bean stuffing to a minimum for best results.

Plan a Sleepover

Invite your friends to spend the night at your house at a special Bean Bag **Friend** Party. Tell your pals to bring nighttime accessories and clothes for your **Friends**. Can you find or make these things for your **Friends**?

- sleeping bag
- little toothbrush
- mini book or diary
- small flashlight
- tiny bag of party snacks
- overnight bag

Finishing Touches

Careful Stitching

Once you are finished stuffing your Bean Bag **Friend**, carefully sew the opening closed. The *slip stitch* is the best stitch to use. Take small stitches close to the edge of the fabric, which loop around the edge of the opening. Try to keep the stitches close together. You don't want the stuffing to fall out!

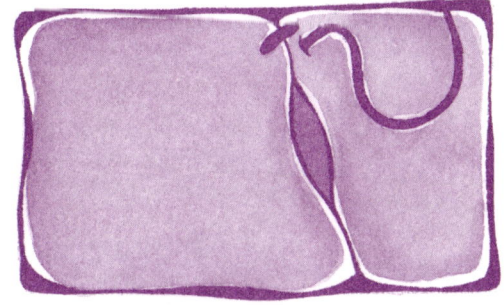

Double Up

The little gap in your Bean Bag **Friends** will be extra strong if you double the thread and knot the two ends together. This also prevents you from losing the thread when you pull the needle away from the fabric.

Starting Off

Each **Friend** has a different personality. Imagine the types of clothes your **Friends** would like. Look through your dolls' clothes for other outfits and accessories that will make your **Friends** more fashionable. Buy some beads, felt, sequins, or other craft supplies at a craft store; or use leftover bits of fabric to sew little hats, skirts, and scarves. Even simple additions like a necktie or a pretty ribbon will look great.

Sample Pattern Layouts
for Careful Cutting

With the materials supplied in the kit you can make three **Friends**. Photocopy or trace the pattern pieces. Remember to copy more than one piece if the pattern says "cut 2 pieces" or "cut 4 pieces". Before you start to cut, lay the patterns on the three pieces of fabric. Then pin the patterns onto the fabric. Follow **Suggestion A** or **Suggestion B** below.

Suggestion A: Bear, Dog, Fish

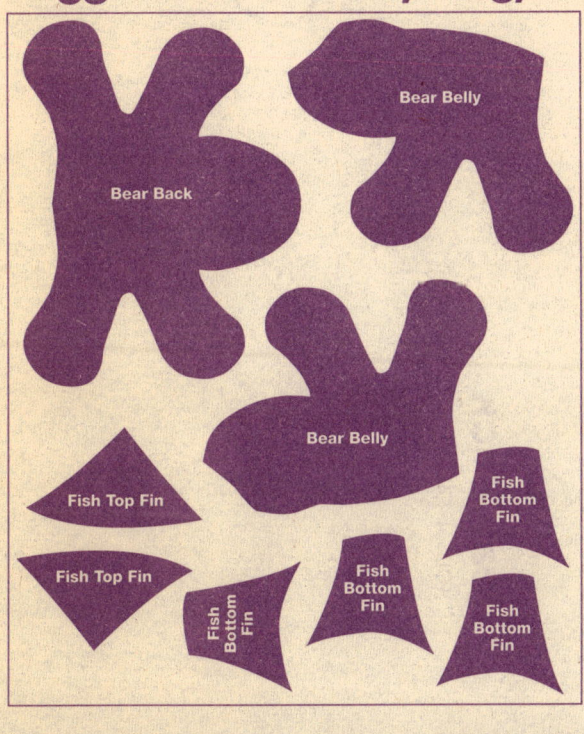
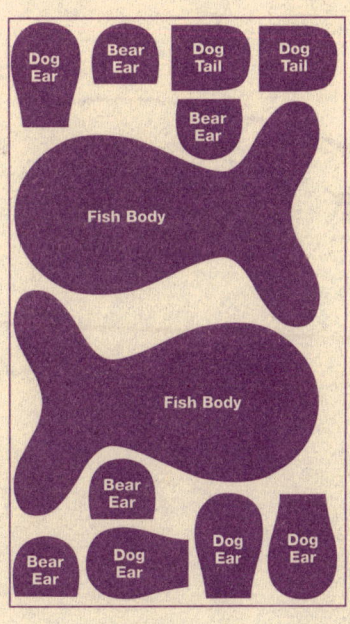
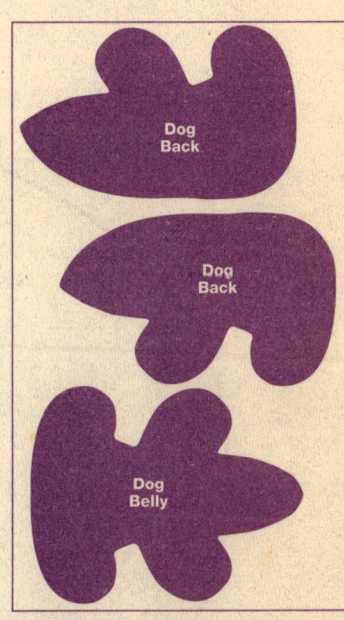

Suggestion B: Frog, Dog, Fish

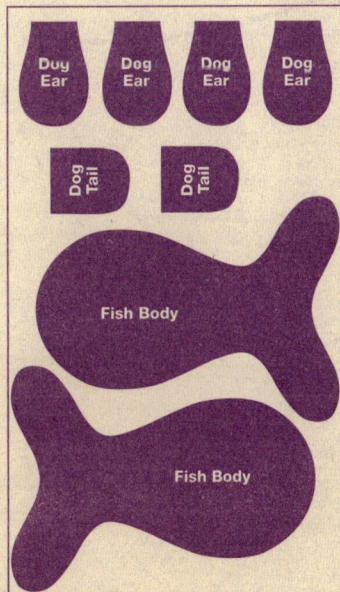
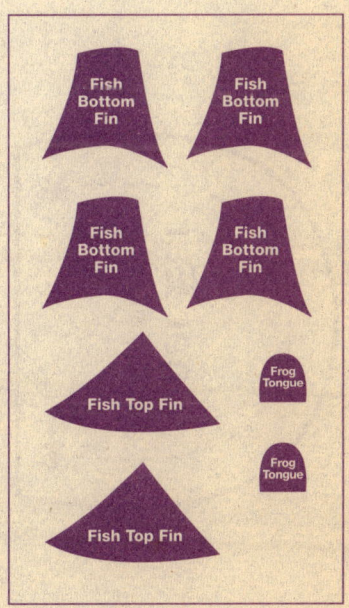

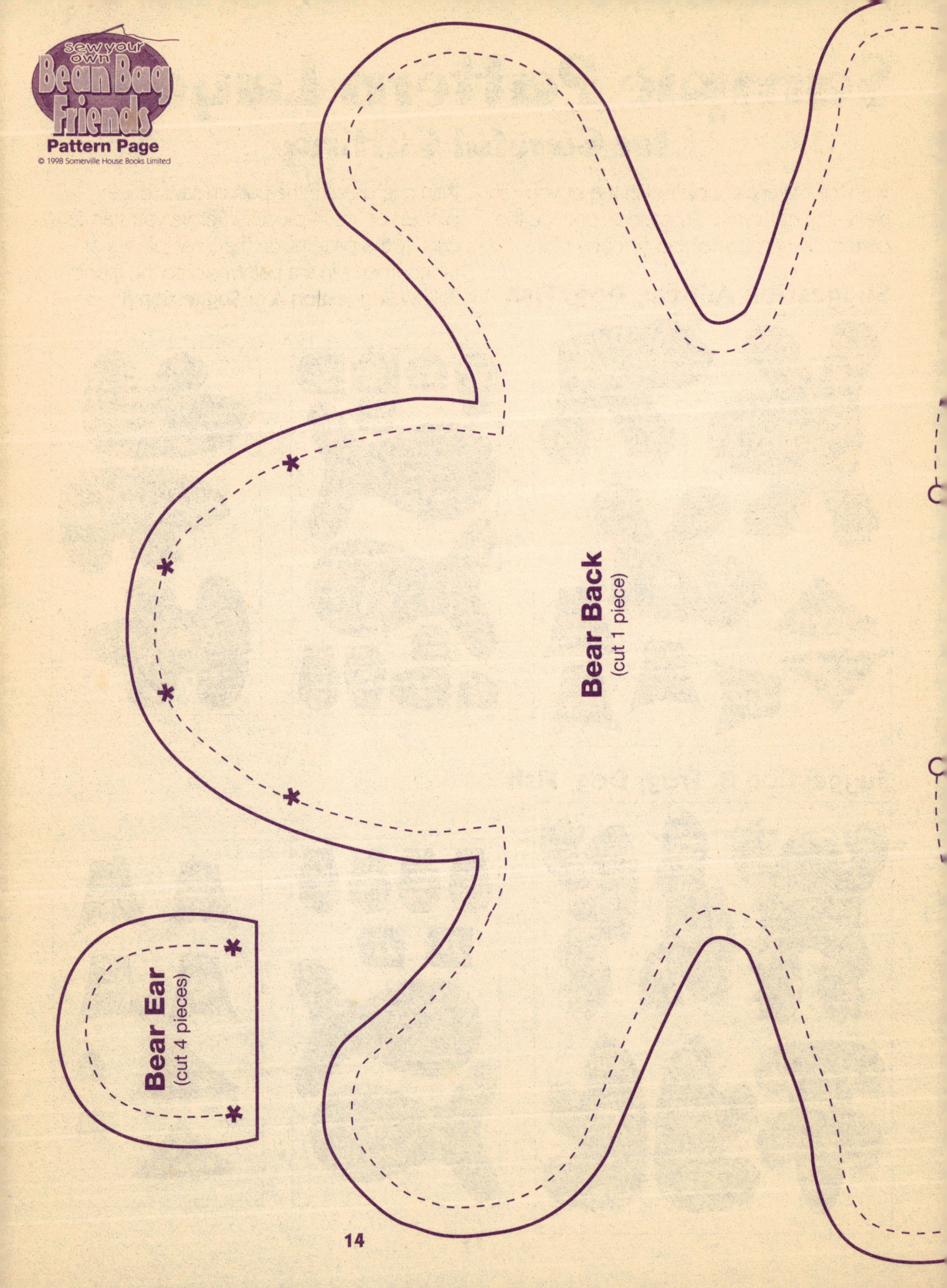

15

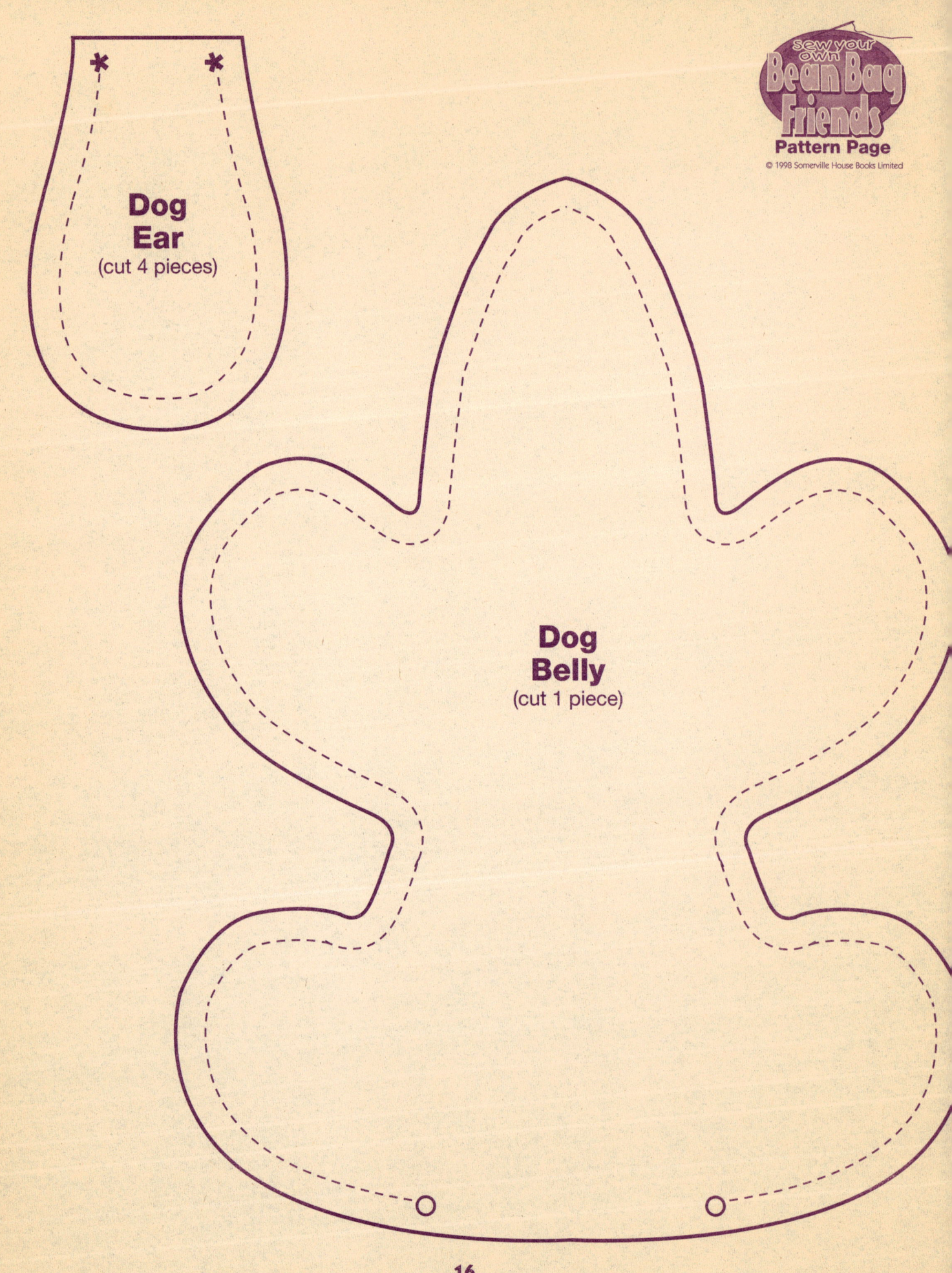

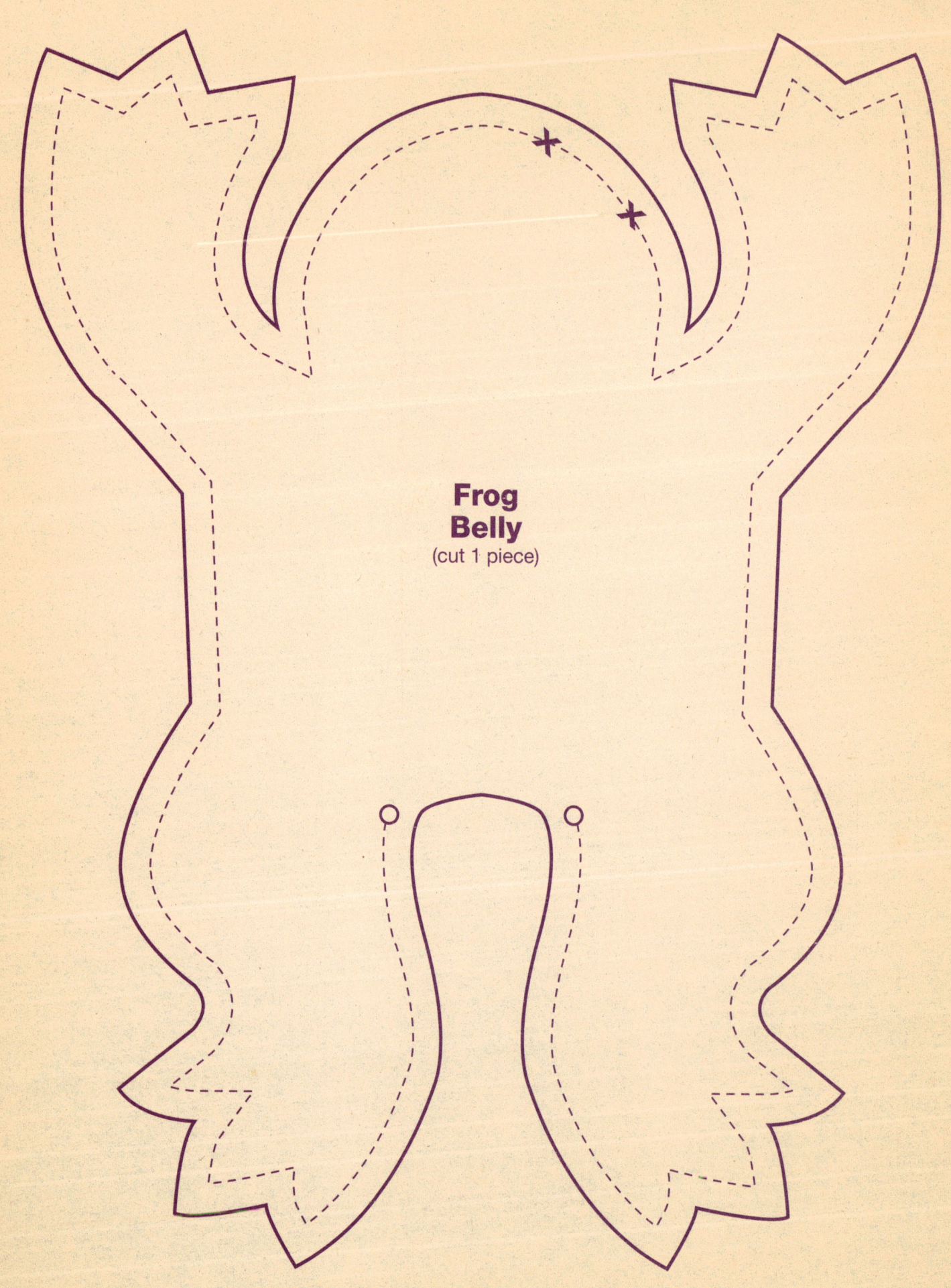

Pattern Page
© 1998 Somerville House Books Limited

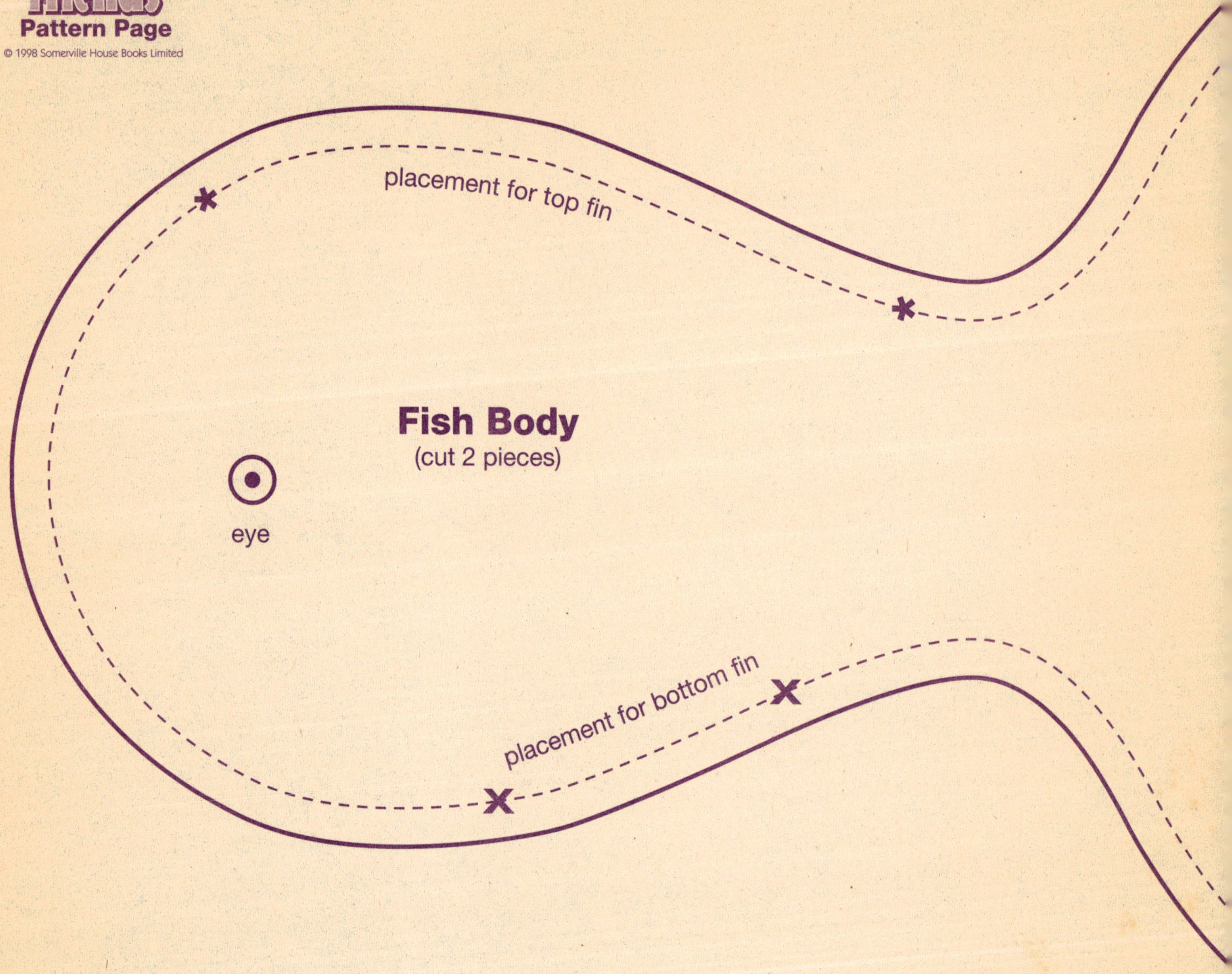

placement for top fin

Fish Body
(cut 2 pieces)

eye

placement for bottom fin

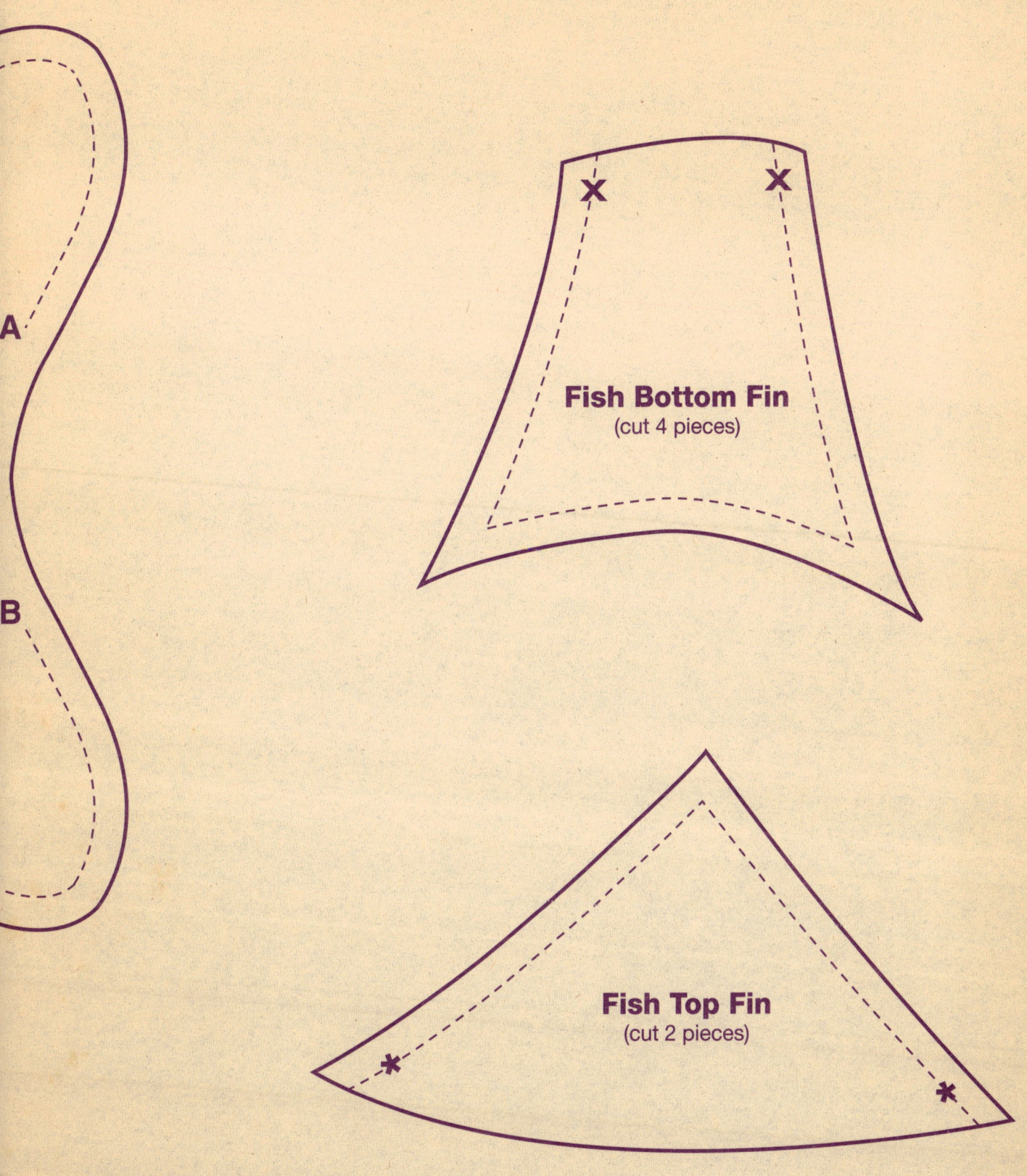

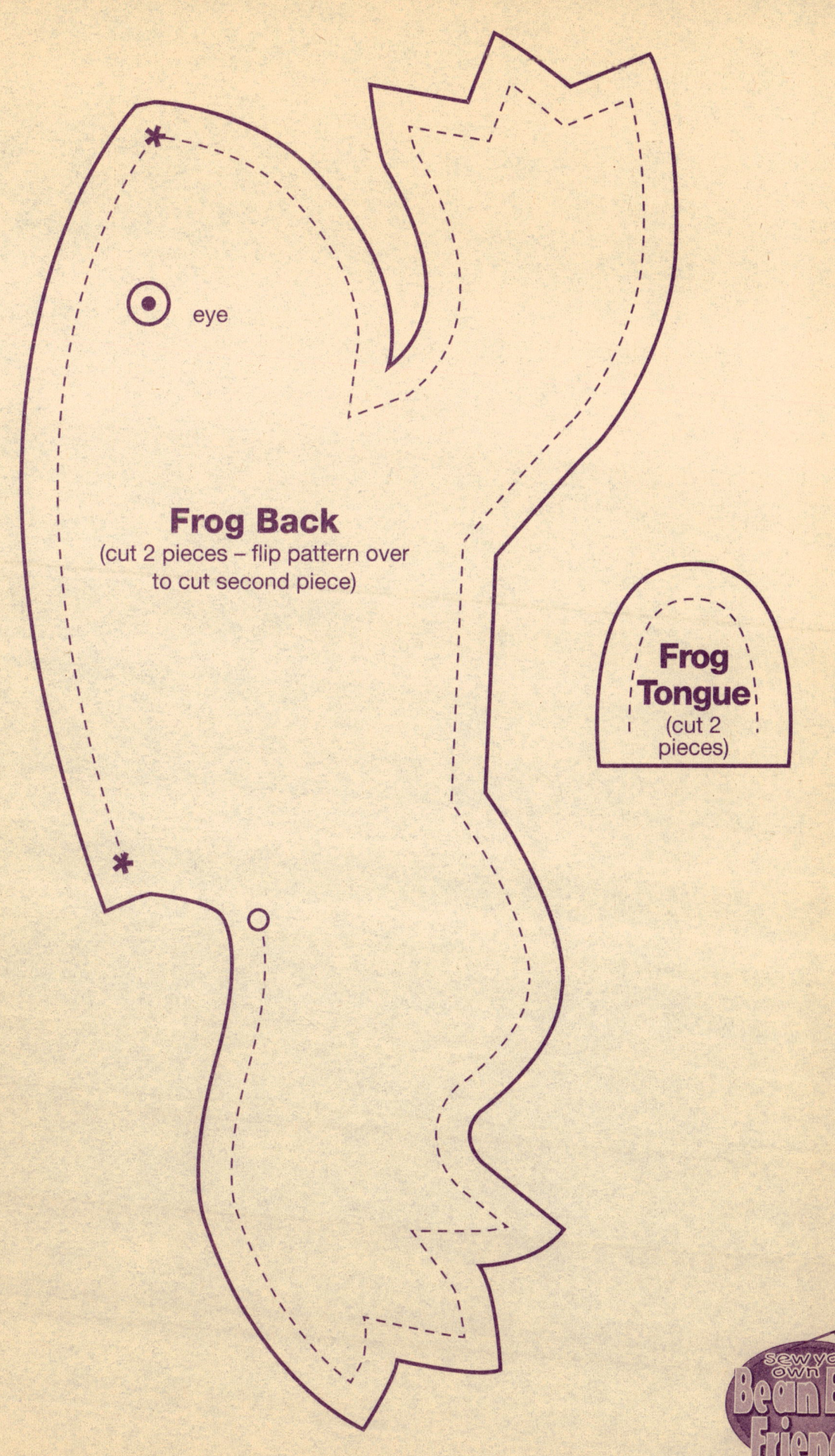

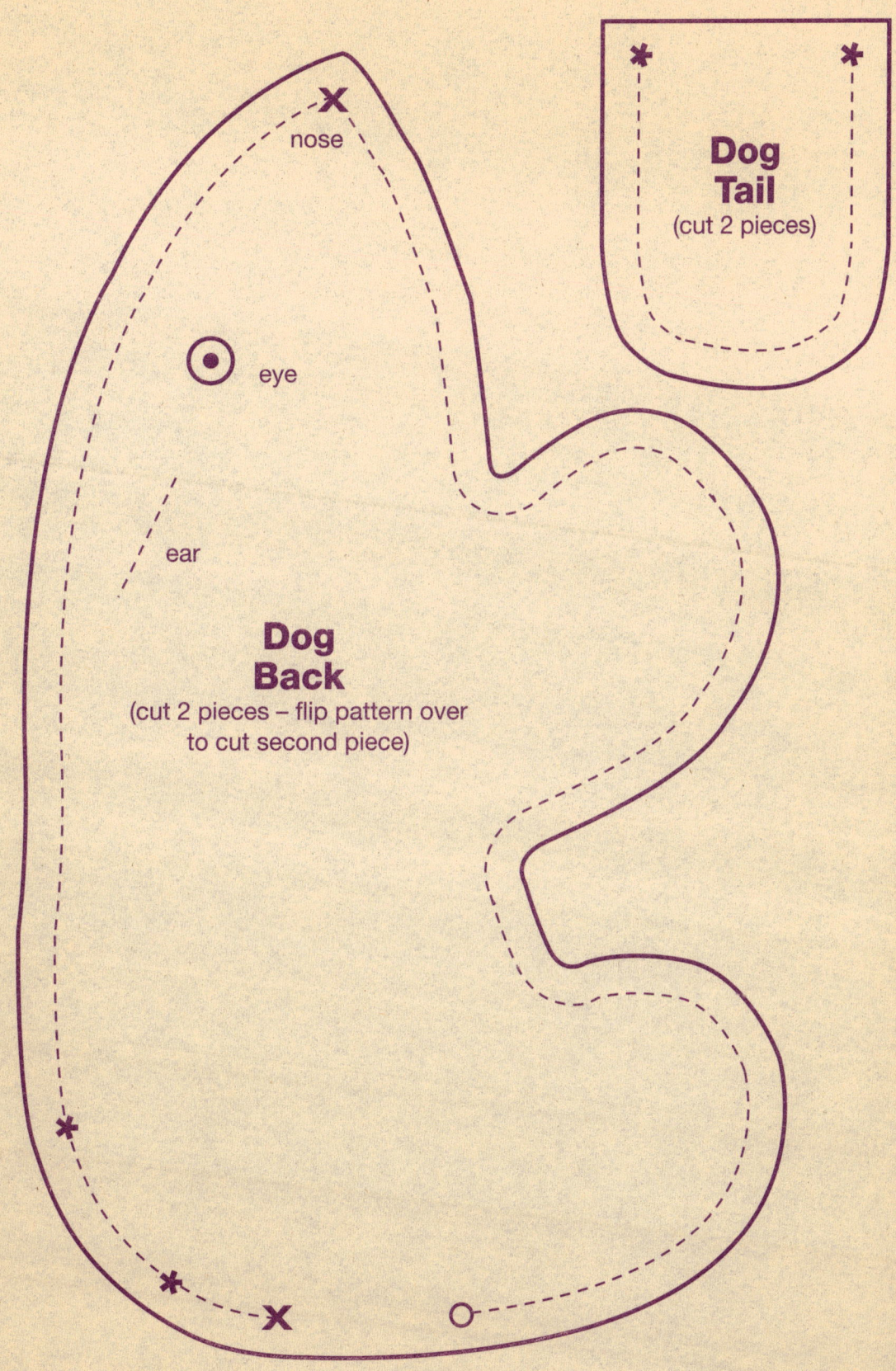

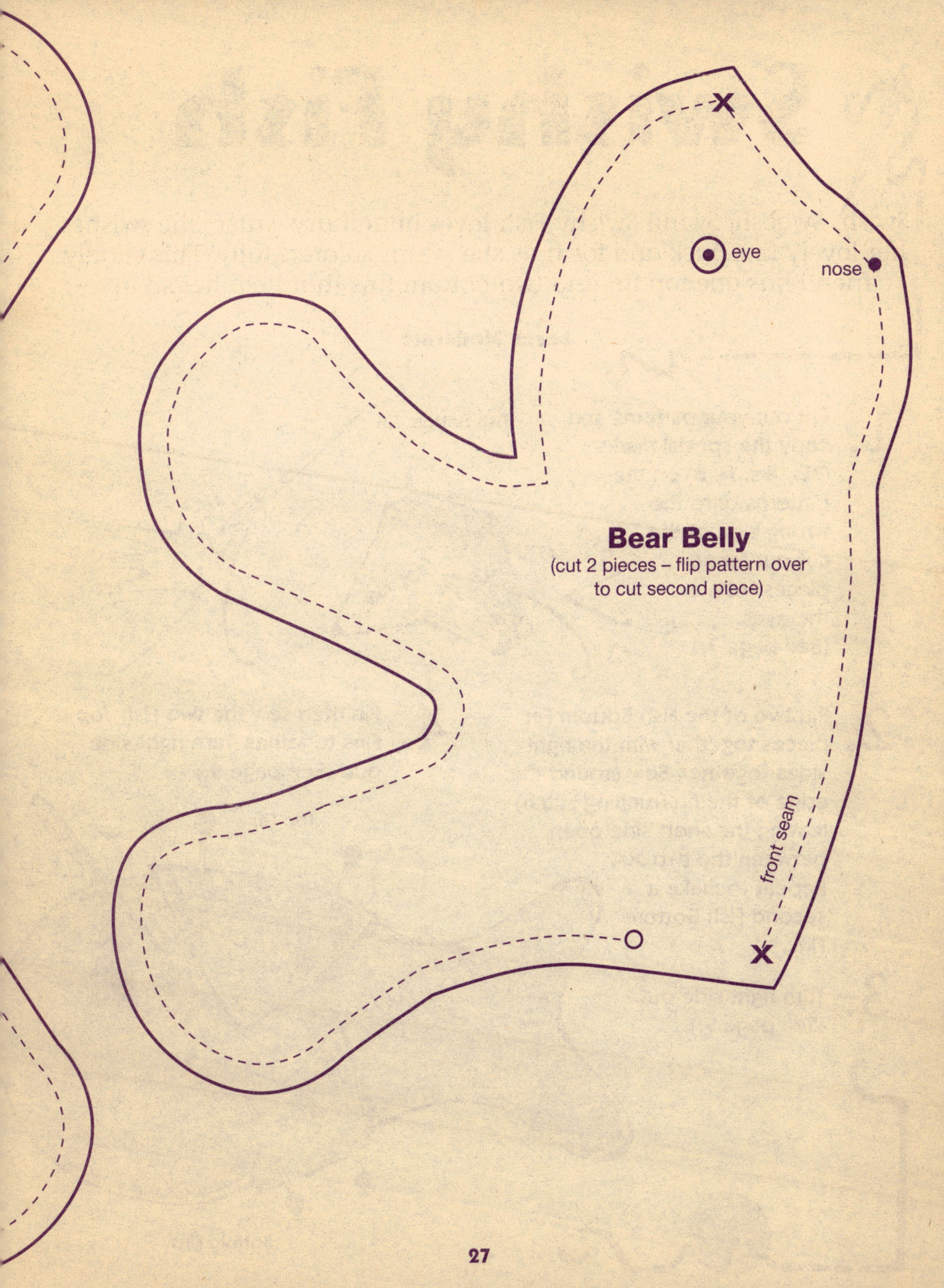

Swishy Fish

Swish, Swoosh, Swim! Swishy Fish loves imaginary water. She swishes her lovely fins back and forth as she swims so gracefully. This cuddly friend has one top fin and two bottom fins that help her sit up.

Level: Moderate

1. Cut out your patterns and copy the special marks (**X**s, **✱**s, **A**, **B**) on the patterns onto the wrong side of the cut-out fabric pieces. Attach the eyes. (See page 7.)

2. Pin two of the Fish Bottom Fin pieces together with the right sides together. Sew around the edge of the fin (running stitch) leaving the short side open between the two **X**s. Repeat to make a second Fish Bottom Fin.

3. Turn right side out. (See page 9.)

4. Pin then sew the two Fish Top Fins together. Turn right side out. (See page 9.)

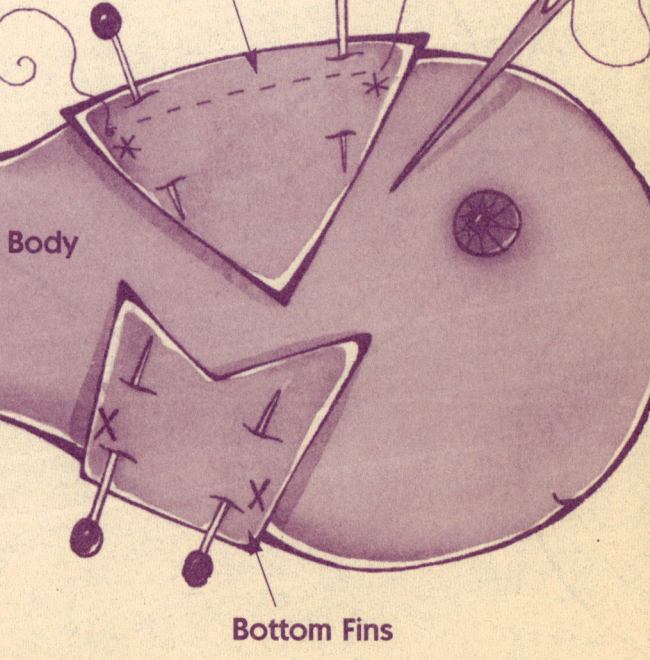

5. Place the bottom fins at **X**s and the top fins at **✻**s, as marked, on one side of the Fish Body.

6. Sew the fins in place. Position the other Fish Body side on top of the assembled unit and pin. The two bottom fins will fit in the same place.

7. Sew all around the outside between the **A** and **B**, as marked. This will leave a 2" (5 cm) gap for turning right side out.

8. Turn right side out. (See page 9.) Now you will see that the fins stick out on the right side!

9. Stuff with beans and sew the opening from **A** to **B** using a slip stitch. (See page 11.) Don't forget to tie the knot!

School Stuff

Braid a little harness for your **Friend** with jute rope or colored yarn. It can hang on the outside of your backpack for all your friends to see. Make a Locker **Friend** to guard your locker while you are in class. You can supply your Locker **Friend** with a backpack, a notebook, sports equipment, or a cool hair style—whatever you like best! If you don't have a locker, make a Study **Friend**.

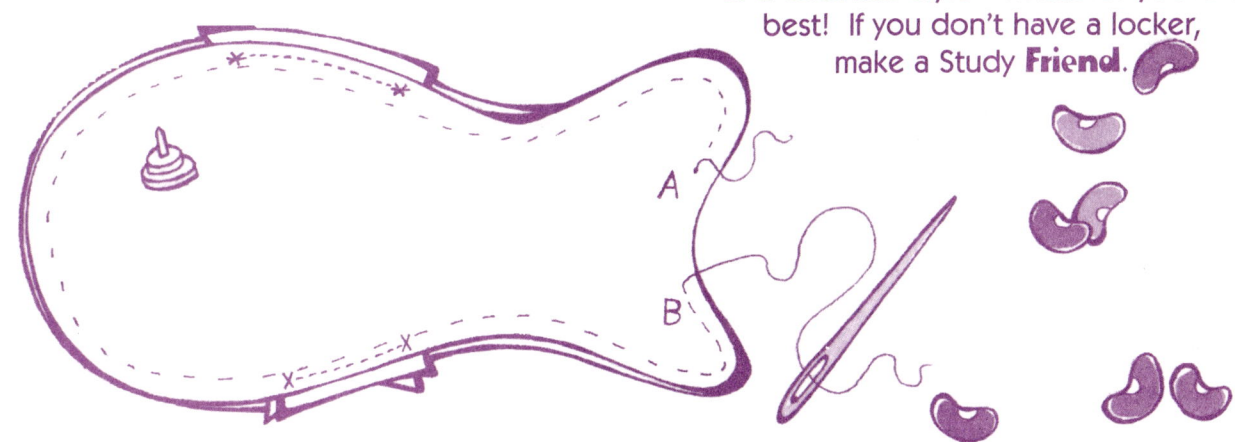

Fernando the Frog

Hippity Hop! Here comes Fernando the Frog! His favorite hobby is gymnastics. Watch him play leapfrog and do the splits. Have you seen any flies lately? Fernando is always looking for a tasty snack.

Level: Moderate

1. Cut out your patterns and copy the special marks on the patterns onto the wrong side of cut-out fabric pieces. Attach the eyes. (See page 7.)

2. Pin the two Frog Back pieces together with the right sides together and sew along the front seam between the two ✱s. See below:

3. Pin the two Frog Tongue pieces together with their right sides together. Sew around the edge of the tongue, leaving the short side open between the two **X**s.

4. Turn right side out. (See page 9.)

5. Place the tongue at the **X**s, as marked, on the Frog Belly. Sew in place.

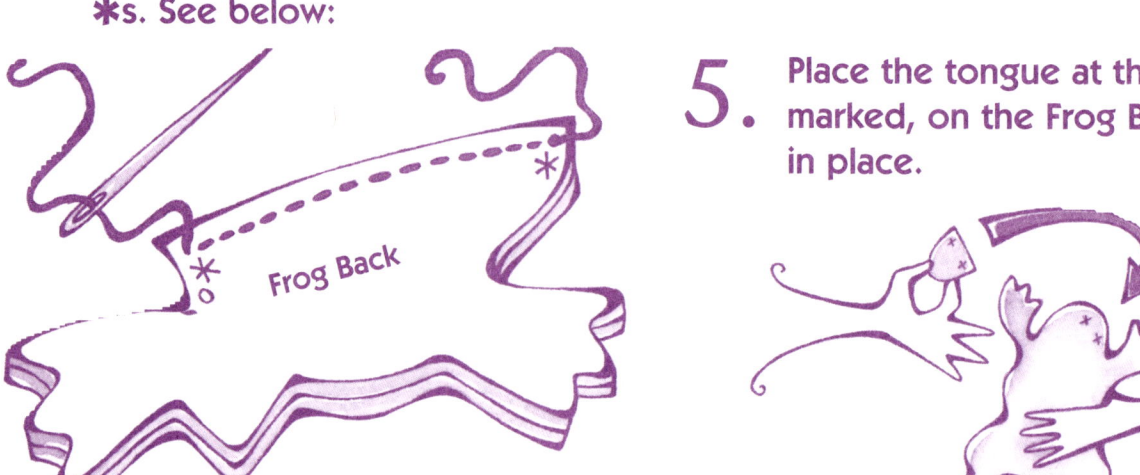

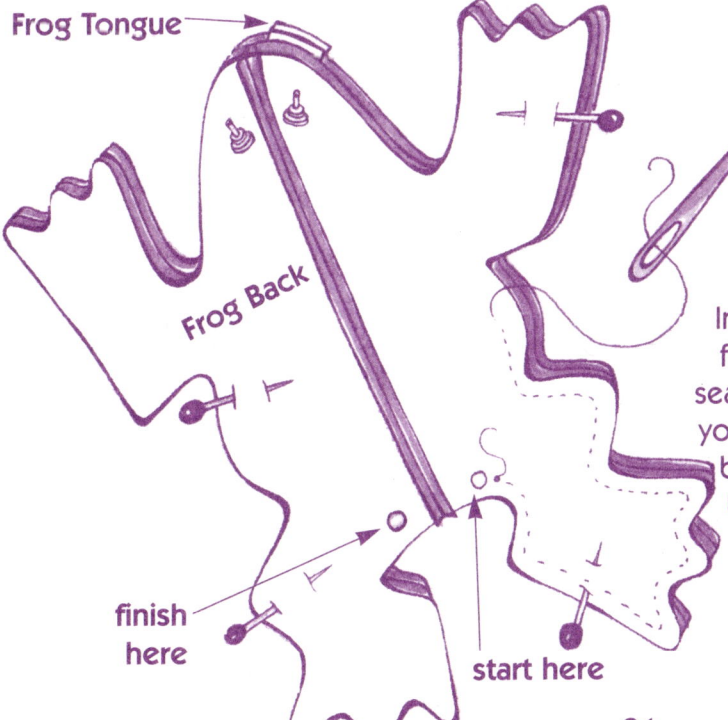

6. With the right sides of the fabric together, pin and sew the Frog Belly to the Frog Back, starting at the O at the frog's leg and continuing around the frog's body to the O on its other leg, leaving a 2" (5 cm) gap to stuff the toy.

7. Turn right side out. (See page 9.)

8. Stuff with beans and sew the opening carefully using a slip stitch. (See page 11.) Don't forget to tie the knot!

Frog Tongue

Frog Back

finish here

start here

Seascape

Invite your friends to bring their frog and fish **Friends**, other stuffed animals, and seashells to create an imaginary seascape in your bedroom. Spread out a blue or green blanket to create a vast ocean. Fill a toy boat with **Friends** and sail to a desert island. Watch out for pirates!

Diggy Dog

Diggy Dog loves being scratched behind his ears. He is good at head-stands, playing dead, and sniffing for his dinner. This winter, Diggy wants to learn to skate! How many triple axels do you think he can do?

Level: More challenging

1. Cut out your patterns and copy the special marks on the patterns onto the cut-out fabric pieces. Copy the **X**s, **O**s, and ✱s to the wrong side of the fabric. Draw the dotted line for the ears on the right side of the fabric! Attach the eyes. (See page 7.)

2. Pin the two Dog Tail pieces together with the right sides together. Pin the Dog Ear pieces, right sides together, to make two ears. Sew around the edge of the Dog Tail and Dog Ears, leaving the short side open between the two ✱s.

3. Turn right side out. (See page 9.)

4. Place the tail at the ✱s, as marked, on one of the Dog Back pieces. Sew the tail in place.

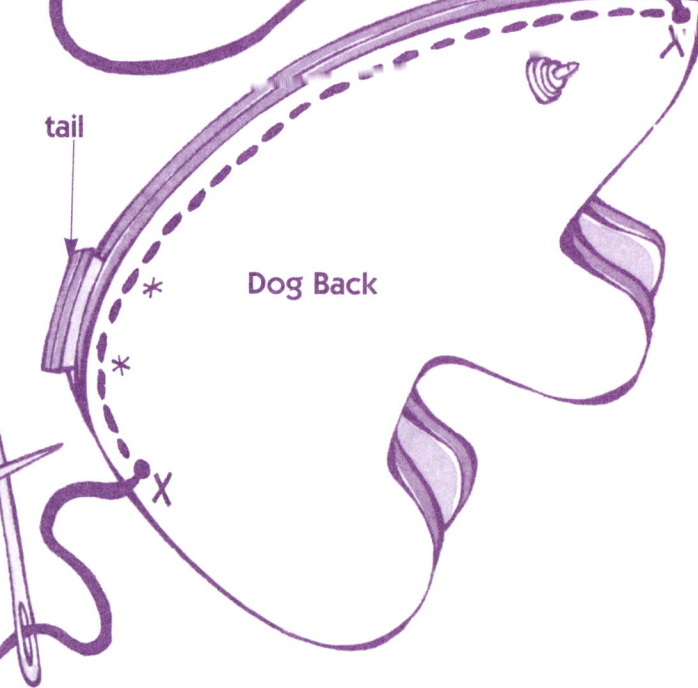

5. Position the other Dog Back piece on top of the assembled unit and pin. Sew the two Dog Backs together between the **X**s.

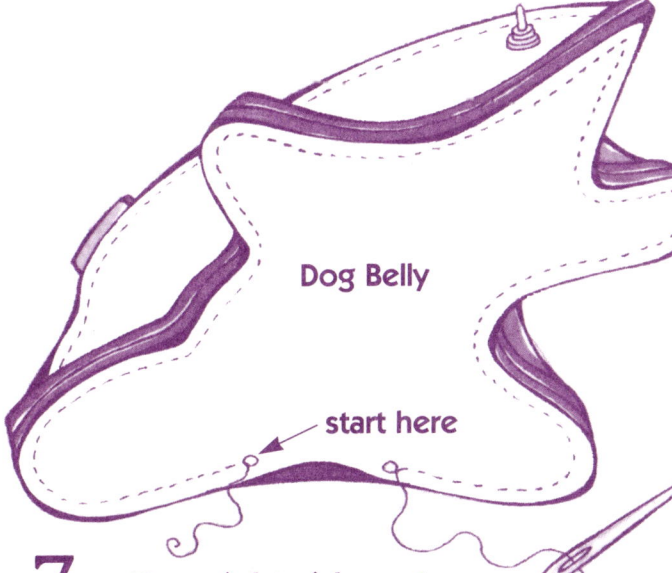

6. With the right sides of the fabric together, sew the Dog Belly to the Dog Back, starting at the ○ on the dog's leg and continuing around the body to the ○ on the other leg, leaving a 2" (5 cm) gap to stuff the toy.

7. Turn right side out. (See page 9.)

8. Attach the plastic nose where the three seams intersect to form the pointed nose.

9. Stuff with beans and sew the opening closed using a slip stitch. (See page 11.) Don't forget the knot!

10. Turn the edges of the open end of the ears inward and sew closed.

11. Sew the ears onto the dotted lines you marked behind the eyes.

Dress Up Diggy

Diggy Dog looks very dapper in a little scarf and a plaid cap. He often goes out of town for skating competitions, so a suitcase would come in handy. You can make one from a small box. Paint it and then decorate it with stickers.

33

Beatrice the Bear

One, two, three—up! Beatrice the Bear climbs trees quickly with her sharp claws. She is looking for a friend in the forest. Who do you think it will be? Snuffle, snuffle, sniff. It's blueberry season! Let's go picking.

Level: More challenging

Extra Material to Find:
- a handful of fiberfill (or you can use a handful of cotton balls held together in the toe of a nylon stocking)

1. Copy the special marks (✘s, Os, ✱s, and nose and eyes) on the patterns onto the cut-out fabric pieces. Attach the eyes. (See page 7.)

2. Pin the two Bear Belly pieces with the right sides together and sew along the front seam between the two ✘s.

3. Pin two of the Bear Ear pieces together with the right sides together. Sew around the edge of the ear, leaving the short side open between the two ✱s. Repeat with second ear.

4. Turn right side out. (See page 9.)

5. Attach the nose.

6. Place the ears at the ✱s, as marked, on the Bear Back piece. Sew in place.

Bear Belly

7. With the right sides of the fabric together, sew the Bear Belly to the Bear Back, starting at the O on the bear's leg and continuing around the Bear Body to the O on her other leg, leaving a 2" (5 cm) gap to stuff the toy.

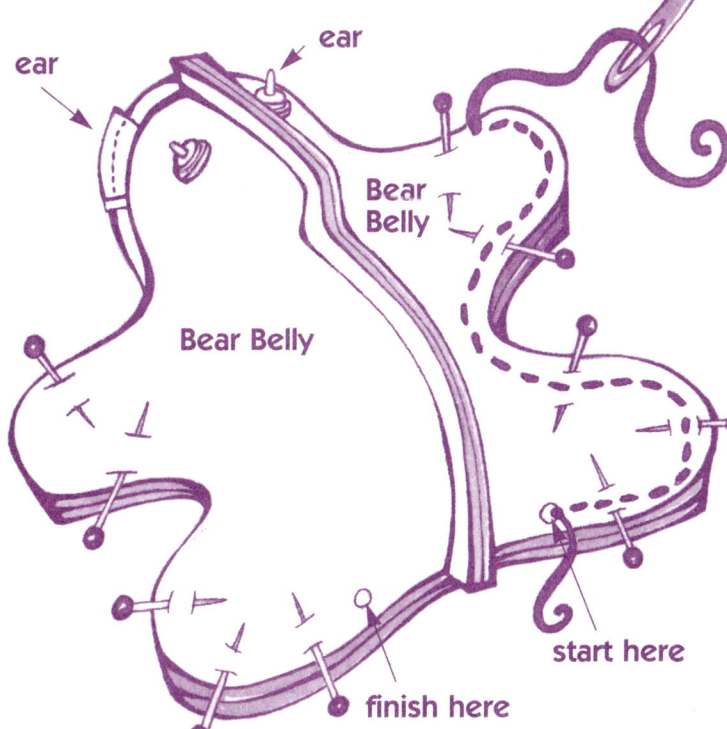

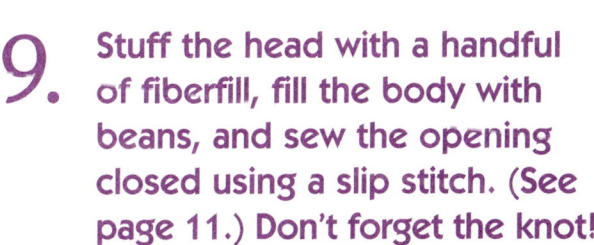

8. Turn right side out.

9. Stuff the head with a handful of fiberfill, fill the body with beans, and sew the opening closed using a slip stitch. (See page 11.) Don't forget the knot!

Plan a Picnic!

Teddy bears love picnics, so why not plan a little party for your friends and their bears? Beatrice loves to dress up for special occasions. Make an elegant hat with a paper doily and tie a satin ribbon around her neck.

Where Do I Sew From Here?

Razzle Dazzle

Friends love jewels. Clip-on earrings, plastic strings of beads, and bracelets all look very attractive on **Friends**. Be creative. Your old bracelet could become a belt for Beatrice. Earrings can decorate Swishy Fish's fins. Diggy Dog would love a star-studded collar. A glittery crown transforms Fernando into a pompous prince.

Buying More Fabric

The best place to buy velour is at large fabric stores. It is a good idea to take your pattern with you when you want to buy more fabric to make another Bean Bag **Friend**. You will need about 1/3 yard (0.3 m) of fabric, depending on the width of the fabric. You might want to take a scrap piece of fabric from this kit along. Other fabrics that will work are Arctic fleece and stretch terry.

Birth Certificates

Fill out these birth certificates for each **Friend**. If you give your **Friend** to a buddy you might want to enclose a card with this important information. This way, you'll be sure your **Friend** receives the best of care.

Special Care

Caring for your **Friends** is fun. Once you know what they like, you will be able to make a good home for them. If their furry skin gets sticky, you can wash the surface with a sponge or a soft cloth and a little soap and water. Scrub the soiled fabric gently. Be careful not to moisten the beans inside.

Don't Wash Me!

Friends should never go in the washing machine or be submerged in water, unless you remove the beans.

The Fun Never Ends

Collect them, show them off, dress them up, decorate them with jewelry, and take them everywhere you go! Bean Bag **Friends** are a delight to everyone. What are you going to make next?

Glossary of Sewing Terms

Arctic fleece	a synthetic knit that is easy to work with; it comes in many colors
fiberfill	soft synthetic material used for stuffing or padding
hand stitch	sew by hand with a needle and thread
notions	thread, eyes, buttons, and feathers; extra things you use when sewing
pattern	a template that shows the pieces needed to make something out of fabric
plush	a thick pile fabric on a knit backing; sometimes called fun fur
right side	the decorated side of the fabric that faces out in the finished **Friend**
running stitch	small, even stitches in hand sewing
seam	a row of stitches that joins two pieces of fabric
seam allowance	the distance between the edge of the fabric and the line you sew along
slip stitch	small, nearly invisible, hand stitches that close up an opening with looping stitches
stitch	a single loop of thread made in fabric by a needle
synthetic fabric	manufactured fiber (polyester, nylon, and acrylic); it tends to be hot in summer and cool in winter when used as clothing
velour	a soft, synthetic, warp-pile fabric often used for bathrobes
wrong side	the undecorated side of the fabric; it doesn't show in the finished product